THE RIGHT WAY TO DRAW ANIMALS

THE RIGHT WAY TO DRAW ANIMALS

Mark Linley

RIGHT WAY

Printed and bound in Great Britain by Cox & Wyman Ltd., Reading, Berkshire.

The *Right Way* series is published by Elliot Right Way Books, Brighton Road, Lower Kingswood, Tadworth, Surrey, KT20 6TD, U.K.

CONTENTS

1

BEGINNING

Many would-be artists believe that drawing animals is a particularly difficult skill. It is not! The secrets in this art medium are knowing how to go about it, and being confident. Don't worry. I will give you confidence and teach you, in easy stages, how to draw animals superbly. I know that by purchasing this book you already have a deep interest in animals, so you are already well under way.

The drawings in this book have been designed so that you can copy them. As you become proficient you will then be able to draw animals from life. This, in fact, is still copying but it requires a little more self-confidence and accurate observation.

My life-long interest in animals began when I was just over four years old. The family lodge reflected hunting in the Far East during the days when wildlife abounded: the sightless gaze of deer and buffalo looked down at me from the walls; glass-eyed leopards' heads stared up from skins on floors; an elephant foot served as a plant pot holder. Wildlife pictures hung everywhere.

I was encouraged by my non-artistic father to draw live looking animals from dead ones. My poor efforts were richly praised and as a result my self-confidence blossomed. Figure 1 is a cartoon of a childhood memory.

Fig. 1 Encouraged to draw animals.

I had my first direct encounter with an exotic live animal a few years later. One day my eccentric father came across a sale of stock from a bankrupt circus. He disappeared inside a huge tent and shortly came out leading two llamas. They were to be pets for my brother and me. On that special day an enterprising newspaper man took a photograph of one bewildered small boy perched astride a frisky llama to which he clung grimly. It was me — and the picture made the front page. At last I was famous! Figure 2 is a quick reminder of this event.

My father seemed not to have given much thought to the problems of keeping two big animals in the back garden of an average sized semi-detached house. The llamas were taken by trailer to our home, however they soon had to be removed to a farm twenty five miles away. I used to look forward to the weekends when we visited our pets. A year or two later the gentle llamas, called Billy and Lady, were given to a zoo.

Now you know why I am interested in animals, why I'm a conservationist, and why I eventually became a wildlife artist.

How to top up your confidence

If you have already read any of my other Right Way To Draw *Paperfront* books (listed on the back cover of this one) you will know how positive thinking will transform your drawing. The following paragraph summarises this for new readers.

What is confidence? My dictionary defines it thus: a firm trust, a feeling of reliance or certainty, sense of self-reliance, boldness. This quality is indispensable for success in any field but how do you achieve it at once? Very easily! You start to think and act positively. How? Simple! You decide you *can*

Fig. 2 My first encounter with a llama.

draw. How does that work? Your conscious thought instructs your wonderful personal computer (your sub-conscious mind) which immediately programs every brain cell towards achieving your object. Beware! When you think "I *can't* draw", your mind does the opposite. Your computer operates just as fast and powerfully on negative instructions!

Positive thinking works like magic. Try it from this moment on. Try it on all things in your life, not simply art.

What you will need

Now that you are brimming with confidence and enthusiasm you can rush round to your local art materials shop for some tools of your new trade. You will need a few drawing pencils graded 2B and 4B (these are soft), and perhaps one H (hard); a soft eraser will be useful; two black ink drawing pens size 0.1 and 0.5, and an A4 size cartridge paper drawing pad or typing paper of the same size complete your initial kit. When you become experienced at sketching animals you could broaden your range by using coloured drawing pencils.

A secret revealed

Finally, before you begin, I would like to share with you my big secret of how to draw animals accurately from life, especially when they are on the move: *look* at your subject for as long as you can. Ask yourself questions. What overall shape is the body? Is it long, curved, oblong or what? Next observe the head. Is it generally wedge-shaped, long, thin, oval or some other shape? Is the face deep, wide, chubby, etc.; are the eyes forward facing or are they placed at the sides? Where do the ears fit? How big are they in proportion? Does the animal have long legs, short, or medium ones? What sort of feet does it have, hoof or paw with four or five claws?

An experienced artist will store a mental note of all this information in seconds. You may take a whole minute! However, you, as a would be artist, must concentrate on the basic *outline* — the silhouette shape — first above all. Instantly you have this fundamental information logged in your computer, start drawing. Stop looking at the animal. Jot down the bare body shape swiftly in the pose you want, walking, feeding, or whatever. Add the neck and head in outline, and the legs and tail in proportion.

Is your silhouette right? Could a friend already recognise what the animal is at once? Go for it again if you need to. Because, no matter how brilliantly you may add smaller detail, you will never capture the animal on paper if your fundamental outline misses the target! Shape up right and your genius will emerge!

Now flash your eyes back to your subject. This time you want to refresh your memory on the small details which you should have purposely waited to attack: you are checking the formation of paw, foot or claw; noting if the tail is spindly or bushy and whether the ears are long, short, or folded flat; observing how nostrils, mouth and jaw come together, and so on. Finally, you can turn your attention to coat markings.

The message is that you can only ever successfully add bit by bit onto a soundly constructed basic shape. This applies equally to people, by the way, as much as it does to animals. Try it by going forward to figure 8 or 9. Choose one; then look at it for three minutes only. Close the book, pop down a basic shape, legs and head; then go back to observe the details. It's all about *looking* accurately.

2

THE FIRST ANIMAL ARTISTS

The simple but accurate drawings of the world's first animal artists are still on the cave walls on which they were drawn many thousands of years ago. They will probably remain as long as our planet survives. Early man had far less intelligence and a smaller brain than ours, so how, then, could he draw the animals around him? Those cavemen who were perhaps instinctively artistic had the ability to make good observations. It was important to them to be able to show others of their tribe what sort of animals were available for food.

Looking properly is vital to all drawing. I do not think that early man was gifted. Drawing is a skill rather than a gift although all professions produce the occasional genius. Early man knew how to *look* — the secret of being able to draw!

Cavemen drew with charcoal (burnt wood), coloured clay, earth, and lamp black from their hollowed-out stone lamps. The home-made paint or ink was applied with hands, fingers or a stick. Think of all the advantages you start with!

In order to teach myself how to draw animals I spent many hours observing and sketching in zoos, wildlife parks and natural history museums. You can learn my skills without doing this. Most of the creatures used as examples in this book are common to town and countryside.

Be an Ice Age artist

Ice age artists left behind many examples of their work,

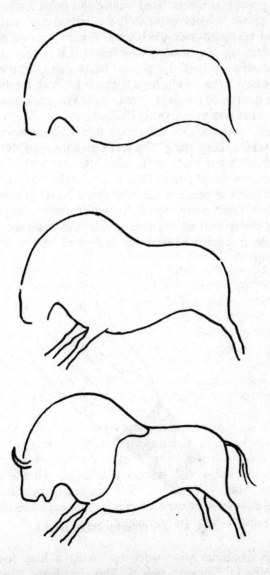

Fig. 3   Try cave art drawing.

some of which was very advanced. The bison was one of their most popular subjects. They hunted this beast for food. It was often drawn in black paint. A few excellent clay models of this animal have also been discovered. Figure 3 shows an Ice Age type drawing of a bison. I have drawn this in easy stages. The top illustration is of the general basic shape. The one below shows how a few details have been added, with the final sketch at the bottom of the page. Notice how few lines there seem to be. I want you to copy this illustration.

First, sharpen your 2B pencil into a chisel point. This is done with a sharp blade. The lead should be made into a wedge shape so that it has a wide edge and also a thin side when turned − a chisel point. This is very useful because you have a dual purpose pencil which will give a broad or thin line. See figure 4. Don't worry about the fact of merely copying at this stage; pretty well all beginner artists start this way. It's useful because it teaches observation and gives help with different techniques.

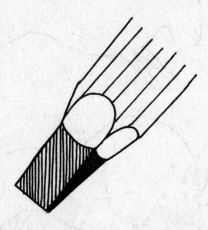

Fig. 4   A chisel pointed pencil.

Now continue your work by taking a long look at the examples in figures 5 and 6. Then, with the same pencil, lightly put down the essential lines of each as you tackle it. When you are happy with these, ink over them using your size 0.1 pen. When it is dry (about one minute) erase only the pencil lines which still show, and admire your handiwork!

The animal shown in figure 5 is called an ibex. It's a goat-like creature which inhabits remote mountainous regions in

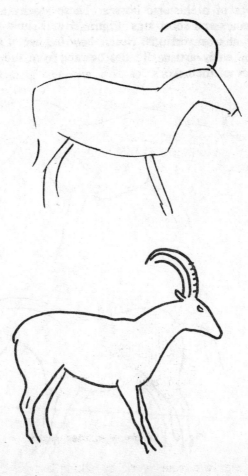

Fig. 5   Draw an ibex.

Europe. The ibex was once very plentiful but is now only found in small numbers. Take a look at the overall shape of the animal. Then try to sketch it quickly and boldly. Remember that once you get the basic shape right you will have a correct structure to work on. Adding the detail of the eye and horn markings will then be quite easy.

In France and Spain there are some remarkable cave drawings of prehistoric horses. These stocky animals had stiff manes and short legs. Figure 6 will show you how to draw your own versions. Notice how the use of so few bold lines by early artists did not detract from the power and accuracy of their work.

Fig. 6   Sketch this Ice Age horse.

Ice Age artists portrayed many other kinds of animal. The mammoth, which we tend to think of as a huge hairy elephant, was smaller than our jumbo of today. Foxes, wolves, bears, lions and reindeer were immortalized on cave walls.

Points to note
1. You can draw better than cavemen.
2. Be bold, confident and enthusiastic.
3. Expect mistakes, they are normal.

3

COUNT SHEEP

You can now move from the Ice Age to the present day for the remainder of this book. I am going to show you how easy it will be for you to draw sheep. You may have noticed, when out of town, how many sheep there are. Thousands and thousands of them graze in meadows, fields, up mountains, almost everywhere. They are all pretty much alike in body shape — only their faces differ. There are white-faced sheep such as the Cheviot, Welsh Mountain, Southdown and Romney breeds, while species of black-faced sheep include the Suffolk, Blackface, Yorkshire and Shropshire varieties.

Oblong with rounded ends

The basic shape of a sheep reminds me of an oblong with rounded ends, added to which are a thin leg at each corner, and a small wedge-shaped head. Once you get this image fixed in your mind you will *always* know how to set about drawing the animal.

The *detailed* shape of an animal can be suggested by the way fur, hair or markings are drawn. The body and limbs are rounded, like our own bits and pieces, so it would be wrong to use straight lines to depict hair or fur. Beginners tend to do just this, and then wonder why their animal appears to be flat sided. It is a help to pencil in lightly half-ovals as a guide. Figure 8 illustrates what I mean.

Pay particular attention to the way I have drawn the wool

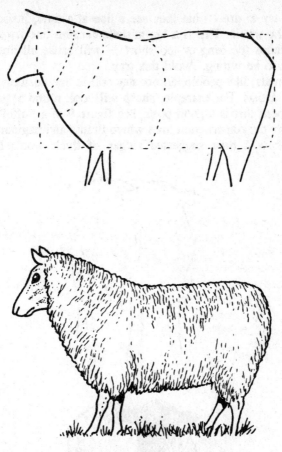

Fig. 8   Oblong with rounded ends.

coat. This was done with small wavy dashes running over the body contours and also down or along the outline of the coat — just the way it grows on the real creature. A few tiny dots on the face and legs denote skin texture. You will find that the humble dot and dash are most useful aids. You will be using this device often. You should find figure 8 quite easy to copy.

Remember to *construct* every one of your drawings from a basic complete outline inwards. This is vital in all work. Many artists try to draw what they see a line at a time, in isolation from the whole. This is a big mistake because one wrong line — perhaps too long or too short — will cause all lines that follow to be wrong. Avoid this trap.

Animals, like people, do not stay still in one position just to please artists. For example, sheep will look round at you. As it happens this is a good pose. See figure 9 of a Suffolk ewe.

Study the construction lines which fit into an imaginary box. Note how I have suggested ridges of thick wool. It isn't

Fig. 9   Draw a Suffolk ewe.

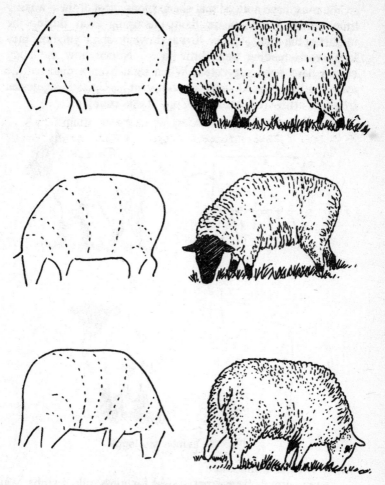

Fig. 10 Draw sheep feeding.

necessary to cover the whole animal with these markings. Indeed, doing that could make the drawing rather boring. All sheep have cleft hooves. Copy this example using my methods. I'm sure that you will achieve a super likeness and raise your own game as a budding artist within a matter of a few moments.

You must have noticed that sheep spend most of their waking time eating. I have heard them chomping away during the middle of the night. Figure 10 was drawn to show you how they look when feeding their little faces. Notice how the body curves have been suggested. When seen from a distance the eyes of a black-faced sheep are not visible. Grass is suggested by short criss-cross strokes. Copy these examples.

Fig. 11 Lambs are leggy.

Lamb without mint sauce

Young animals have great appeal for most folk. Lambs, you will be pleased to learn, are far easier to draw than children! Little lambs have long legs, undeveloped coats and rounded heads. It is amazing how a beautiful little lamb quickly grows into a cumbersome over-weight adult. (After mature sheep are sheared they become, once more, leggy animals.) See how the rounded bodies of little lambs are suggested in figure 11. Draw your own versions of these.

Get close

A good animal portrait makes an attractive picture. I have chosen the handsome ram's head used as an emblem by Yorkshire National Park for the sketch in figure 13. It is not wise to approach a ram closely. It might take exception to having you on its territory. They are very powerful animals. I was once charged by a young ram but escaped injury by leaping onto the top of a large bale of straw! Take no chances: observe them, as I do, from behind a wall, fence, hedge or in a cattle market.

Take a careful look at figure 12. See how the construction lines must be accurate before details are added. Your problem here is to draw the horns correctly. In many rams the two horns do not match each other. My example shows this. Sketch, in pencil, the wedge-shaped face before putting in the curly horns. Start as in the top illustration in figure 12. Then add the outlines of where the dark patches are to go. See the lower illustration. Pencil in the nostrils, mouth and eye.

Now go to figure 13 to see how all the shading is done. The optical illusion of round horn is obtained by using curved lines to suggest the form. Put in a few battle scars over and around the curved lines. The dark patches of hair are best created by making scores of tiny lines which follow the direction they grow on the animal. You will need to look carefully in order to get this right. Pop in a few lines in the white areas. Draw the long body hair as straggly streamers which point downwards. Sketch in the eye. Cast a critical look over your drawing then start to ink it in. This advanced picture will take a little time. I feel sure that you will manage it. Make space on your sideboard for your little gem!

Go for it

I once came across a group of pretty creatures called Jacob's sheep. These are an ancient breed which are now gaining popularity. The lambs had black blotches against pure white. The adults had patches of dark brown. I sketched the original for figure 14 after watching them for half an hour.

I want you to copy this scene by working out for yourself the

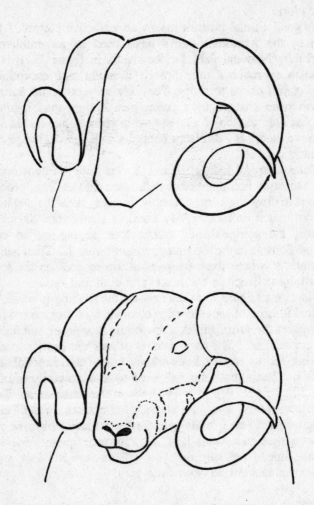

Fig. 12 The first construction lines.

different basic shapes of the animals. Once you have done this correctly, in pencil, the drawing is quite straightforward. Pay particular attention to the curved back of one lamb, the stocky legs, shoulder blades, and rounded head. The standing lamb is

Fig. 13   The finished ram drawing.

nibbling the ear of its twin. Mother, in the background, keeps her eye on them. You will use lots of dots and dashes as shown in my drawing. When your pencil sketch is complete draw over it with a size 0.1 pen. This is an ambitious picture but there is nothing in it which you can't do. Your finished masterpiece could make a nice greetings card for your spouse, friend or bank manager! Go for it!

Assignments
1. In ink or pencil draw any animal from a photograph.
2. Choose an animal from this chapter. Look at it for three minutes. Close the book then quickly draw it. Check your result.
3. Try the same system working from a live animal. It could be a pet dog, cat or a sheep.

Fig. 14 Draw these Jacob's sheep.

4

BE UP TO SCRATCH
WITH CATS

This chapter is devoted to teaching you how to draw the type
of cat found in every village, town and city in this country: the
short-haired domestic moggie which is also popular the world
over. If you can sketch a cat accurately then you will be able
to draw any creature. It is the pet most frequently drawn by
beginner artists. We shall spend extra time learning how to
depict this fascinating animal.

Cats of all kinds are my favourite animal subjects. I like to
watch them, stroke them, talk to them, draw, paint and sculpt
them. The graceful way they move gives an impression of
hidden power. A flexible coat and spine allows them to adopt
a wide range of interesting poses.

The hardest problem solved

When you can correctly draw a cat's face you have solved
the hardest part of the job. Many people go wrong here because
a cat's skull structure is not easy to fathom at first glance. The
bone formation is hidden by muscle and fur. If your first cat
picture resembles a lop-sided plum pudding with eyes and ears,
don't worry — you are about to bring your cats up to scratch!

Unlike dogs, all cats have a similar face. Once you can draw
cats you should be capable of portraying their big relations,
tigers, lions, leopards and right through the 37 species of the
feline family.

Like millions of other people I have a pet cat. She adopted me when she was a five month old stray kitten. She knew a mug when she saw one! It is likely that our domestic cat is descended from ancestors who lived in ancient Egypt 4,000 years ago. Cats were then deemed to be gods and treated as such. My own pet seems aware of this, judging by the way she demands instant attention and easily manipulates me into obtaining exactly what she wants.

I have reminded her that in Medieval days the Church, quite wickedly, pronounced all cats to be devils. My moggie dismissed this bit of history with an imperious look and angry twitch of her tail. She probably knew that, as a result of one silly Pope's decree, cats were cruelly persecuted for years; this happened despite cats being worth their weight in gold during the Great Plague, which was caused by millions of rats. I call my pet, TC (Top Cat). We shall use her as a model for many of the exercises that follow.

Figure 16 shows some quick sketches of TC. Examine the two profiles. The 3-dimensional feel is achieved sparingly by adding fur, first put in with dotted lines.

See the way the ears have been drawn. A cat's ear has a thick ridge round the base at the rear, as shown in the lower illustration.

Observe how small and delicate the nose is and how cats always seem to be smiling due to a gently curved mouth line. The lower jaw fits snugly into the top jaw.

Most cats have white whiskers but you can depict these with fine black lines. There are a group of six whiskers over each eye, and four or five rows on each side of the mouth. You don't want to put all of them in, just a few will be enough.

My cat has a pronounced forehead. This feature varies slightly from cat to cat, as does the length of the nose. In this respect animal faces are like human faces. Every one is unique to its owner. TC has a short nose. She was dozing when I first sketched her, so her eyes were closed. In my second profile you can see TC doesn't miss a trick when her eyes are open! Cats, by the way, spend three quarters of their lives asleep or resting. This is good for artists!

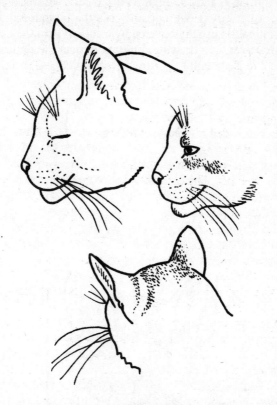

Fig. 16   A close-up of a cat's head.

To begin with, leave out detailed fur. I return to help you with that shortly. You will also help yourself by making all your drawings larger than the printed versions can be in this book. Copy figure 16 carefully. It is a key to drawing all cats well.

Drawing a cat's face from the front should not give you any more trouble than a profile sketch — once you learn where each feature should go. The most common errors I see beginners make include drawing the cat's nose too big and the ears perfectly triangular, which they are not. In fact they are petal-like in structure with curved ends. There is a small kink at the base of the outer rim. Newcomers to art tend to draw the eyes too large and too high in the face. There is black skin round a cat's eyes. We normally see the bottom half of this. The top half is usually covered by a fold of skin – a cat's eyelid. However, in a drawing, little more than the outline shape of the eye is enough to portray it without excess detail intruding.

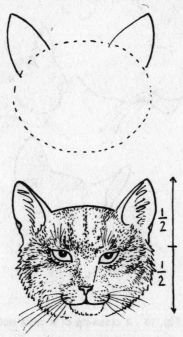

Fig. 17 How to get proportions correct.

Study figure 17. Notice that the basic shape is oval. The ears are elliptical. Roughly half way between ear tips and bottom of the lower jaw is where the eyes look out. Half way between the eyebrows and lower jaw line is where the *top* of the nose is. With a little practice you will soon automatically get these proportions right. Copy this example in pencil; then ink it in. Practise drawing some more cat heads from life, from books or from your photo album until you can do them from memory. This will be a big advance for you.

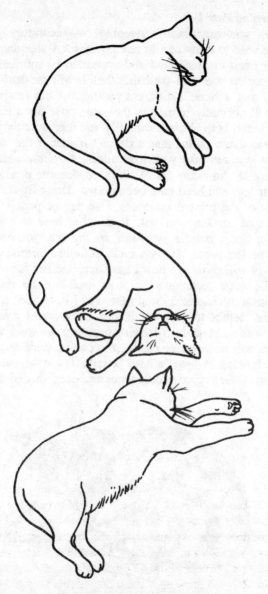

Fig. 18 Sleeping positions.

Let sleeping cats lie

When you can draw a sleeping cat accurately you will then be able to draw one in any position. A sleeping moggie may be deep in dreamland and appear to be motionless, but no sooner do you start sketching than it will suddenly twitch, stretch, and assume a different position! A cat resting, however, will normally remain in the same pose for a long time.

The secret is to observe carefully and then quickly jot down the basic shape. After that it doesn't matter if the cat moves because you can take your time adding the little details.

Figure 18 shows my cat TC in three sleeping positions. See how her legs and head have been drawn. Draw figure 18 twice the size of the printed examples. Use pen or pencil.

Put coat markings in last. Remember how to convey the curve of body, muscle and limb, by the way you make your marks on the paper. TC is a multi-coloured tortoiseshell cat. Figure 19 will show you how I have depicted her fur markings. It is the same technique that was used for the ram's head illustration in chapter 3. Study the way I have used fine lines, dots and dashes to give an illusion of different colours and tones. With most modern drawing pens you can work very fast. The ink will not smudge easily. You can produce an excellent pencil drawing by using a hard pencil (H) for the outline then a soft one (4B) to give middle tones and deep shades. Beautiful

Fig. 19 Dots and dashes depict coat markings.

pencil drawings are quite rare. Don't ignore this medium which, in fact, is easier than pen work. Copy figure 19. In this pose she was sitting on her tail which can just be seen poking between her hind legs. If your drawing goes wrong, don't worry. Look again and then re-draw. It pays to be determined and patient.

Fig. 20 A watching cat.

Watch it watching

As mentioned previously, a cat spends much of its time resting. My pet, for example, will stay in a comfortable position for ages if she is watching her territory from the vantage point of a window-sill inside the kitchen. Figure 20 gives the rounded basic shapes which combine to make up the outline drawing. The lower illustration shows TC when she looks round to see what I'm up to. Copy these sketches in pencil or pen. Fill in the fur details in the top illustration.

A friend's pet was used as a model for figure 21. She is a large tabby with a nice gentle disposition. The markings on her coat were created in the same manner as for figure 19. She has very dark markings along her back, her stripes are black and her face and chest are white. Draw your version of this tabby cat. Although you are copying my work your efforts will not be exactly like mine. This is good because you are developing your own unique style. You could become the best cat artist in the world!

Fig. 21 Draw a tabby cat.

Clean cats

Cats spend a good deal of their time grooming. They are one of the cleanest animals around. They always follow the same procedure when having a wash and brush up: they begin with

Fig. 22 Wash and brush-up poses.

their paws; then comes the head, followed by flanks, body and the tail last of all. During their ablutions they make many interesting shapes. Figure 22 shows you some grooming

Fig. 23   Draw a little tiger.

positions. Draw a page or two of these, and have a shot at
putting in the markings as I have done in the top sketch. Make
your studies larger than mine.

Moving moggies

Moggies on the move are graceful creatures. At times they
go like lightning, much too fast for our eyes to see. Figure 23
was drawn from a quick sketch made when I saw a visting little
tiger in my garden. See, as *always*, how the basic shape was
first jotted down before finishing the drawing. The stripes were

Fig. 24 Draw an angry cat.

put in with a size 0.5 pen. All the tiny dots are drawn with a 0.1 pen.

My moggie seems to hate others of her kind though she likes people. She will normally attack any moggie who enters her territory. The battle is usually short and sharp. Fur flies everywhere but it isn't hers! I once watched her as she confronted a dog fox who trotted down the garden path. She transformed herself by puffing out her fur. Her tail closely resembled that of the fox. She hissed loudly. The fox cautiously walked round her then went on its way. Figure 24 is my impression of an angry cat. See how you get on with this one.

Fig. 25   Draw this kitten.

Kittens are popular

Kittens, like all baby animals, have a lot of appeal and are very popular subjects with the buying public. Kittens seem to have huge ears. This is because they grow slower from birth than the rest of the head and it seems to be nature's way for them to start proportionally larger. Have a look at the kitten in figure 25. Build a basic shape from this, then make a finished drawing. It should be good enough to make a little present for your favourite cat person. Tackle the portrait of the long-haired kitten in figure 26 next. Notice the large eyes and ears. The long fur is best drawn with quick, loose strokes. Try it.

Fig. 26 A long-haired kitten.

Assignments
1. From life or photographs draw three different cat heads.
2. Do the same with complete cats.
3. Watch a cat for a while. Then look down at your drawing pad and capture the outline shape with deft strokes. Check your effort by looking at your subject again. Now tackle detail such as face, tail and claws. You can sneak another look whenever necessary. Finally, draw the fur markings.

5

RABBIT, RABBIT, RABBIT

Rabbits, bless them, are delightful animals which are common throughout our countryside. It is just as well for them that they breed so freely. Thousands of little bunnies provide a tasty snack for fox, weasel, stoat, and birds of prey. In addition to its natural enemies the species is constantly persecuted by man. It remains, nevertheless, a much loved animal by children and many adults.

It's all in the head

After your work on chapter 4 you will find that rabbits are much easier to sketch than are cats. Once again, the most common error made by beginner artists is in portraying the head. There is an easy way of drawing this correctly. Look at figure 28. The top sketch shows a rough pear-like form. The middle illustration has this shape more clearly defined by four straight lines of different lengths. This is the correct format for a rabbit's skull. Fix this in your mind. Then draw it from memory. The lower drawing has been completed by added details. The straight lines are now not quite so straight. See how the eye, nostril, petal-like ears, fur and whiskers have been depicted. I used a size 0.1 pen for this. Copy figure 28 in either pen or pencil.

When you can draw this head shape accurately you will be well on the way to sketching all animals that have a similar skull shape: hares, squirrels, mice and others.

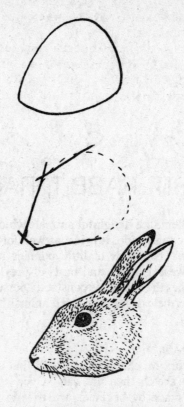

Fig. 28   Construct a rabbit's head.

Start with the young

Young rabbits are easy to draw. They have oval bodies, small ears, and heads like those you have just drawn. When rabbits are very small they seem to be happy creatures unafraid of man. By keeping still you can observe them at close quarters for long spells of time. Figure 29 was drawn to show you how to make the basic outlines and then go on to finish your drawings of young rabbits. The fur texture was put in as dot stipple with a size 0.1 pen. The best way of doing this is to hold your pen in a relaxed grip and bump it quickly up and down on the paper. You simply do more dots where you want the deepest tone or shadow, and few where you want white or reflected light to show.

You can get a good picture in pencil alone with the advantage that a background tone is possible. Use a grade HB for the outline then a 2B for putting in background tone. The tone is done by *rubbing* the 2B lead on to a piece of scrap paper

Fig. 29   The basic shape of young rabbits.

covering an area, say, of a postcard, and then taking it off with a bit of clean cloth which you use to transfer it onto the area you wish to cover. This way avoids having any pencil strokes showing. Once you add your dot stipple with an HB pencil to achieve the look of real fur, with dots, short dashes and lines, the resulting bunny will look more realistic than a pen sketch. By using two or more pencil grades a wide range of tones is possible. This simple technique can be applied to all animal subjects and to many landscape backgrounds. Try copying figure 29 in pencil and pen. See how different each medium is. Notice how the head outline slightly overlaps the body oval.

Fig. 30   Draw basic shapes first.

Your next task is to work out the basic outlines of the rabbits drawn for figure 30. Use a larger scale than used here. (How to enlarge drawings is dealt with in the last chapter.) When you have done this, put in all the details. Work in pen, pencil or both.

Adult rabbits

As a rabbit grows to become an adult some features naturally change from those it had as a kitten (the correct term for baby bunnies). We need to be acutely aware of these differences when drawing them. The hind legs are larger and more powerful; the ears are longer and usually black-tipped; the tail is slightly bigger and is black on the top and pure white underneath. (This is used as a warning sign to others of its

Fig. 31   Adult rabbits.

Fig. 32   Sketch this bolting rabbit.

kind.) Rabbits are rather cat-like in the way they groom themselves, sit, rest, and are given to sudden bursts of fast movement.

Study figure 31 and then copy it. First draw the basic shape before progressing to the finished illustration. A rabbit bolting from danger moves very quickly. Its head is held back with ears laid low along the back. The tail is high to signal possible impending disaster. You can see what the legs do by looking at figure 32. Copy this example to a larger scale; then put in fur detail.

Draw rabbits from life

The very best way of learning how to draw is to get out, observe, then quickly jot down what you see on your sketch pad. Almost all the drawings in this chapter were from sketches that I made on one trip in the countryside. I found a

Fig. 33   Sketch from life.

large field which was enclosed by tough wire-mesh fencing used to safeguard petrol storage tanks. The place was a haven for rabbits. Their enemies could not easily get at them.

I watched rabbits of all ages enjoying a spring afternoon. Some were feeding, others grooming; a few loped about whilst comrades rested or slept. Accurate basic outlines were what I wanted. No details were drawn at this stage. Close-up views were obtained by squinting through lightweight binoculars. In less than an hour I had more than enough rabbit shapes to work from. Figure 33 is of rabbit outlines. Draw a few or all of these to a larger scale. Then put in fur texture using the techniques I have given you. Next time you visit rabbit territory take a small drawing pad and do the same exercise.

The handsome hare

The hare is very similar in structure to a rabbit. It has the same sort of skull shape with longer hind legs and ears. You may have seen these handsome animals boxing each other, balancing on their hind legs. This is a courting routine that begins in early spring and can continue for several months. Hares are found in uplands and where there is hilly meadow land. It's a great pity that this animal is still hunted by so-called sportsmen in areas where numbers have dwindled almost to extinction. They simply worsen the losses caused by changes in agriculture over recent decades. Where excessive hare populations obliterate crops may be another matter.

Figure 34 will show you how to draw the head and body of a hare. There are no new problems for you with these. Draw them in pencil or ink.

The only defence a hare has against its enemies is its speed. The powerful hind legs have evolved to make it move uphill at a great pace. A hare will always try to escape danger by galloping up a hill rather than down. Figure 35 of a hare in flight will give you the idea of how to draw it in action. Have a go at this but make it bigger than the printed version. Draw in some fur detail.

Fig. 34 How to draw a hare.

Assignments

1. Choose a drawing of a rabbit from figure 33. Look at it for one minute. Close the book and draw it from memory. Check your work. Repeat this exercise with several more poses. This is wonderful practice for becoming good at drawing from life.

Fig. 35 A hare in flight.

2. Draw a life-sized portrait of a rabbit from a photograph or from life.
3. Draw a hare from a picture, or from life.
4. If you can take a telephoto snapshot of, or capture on video, a leveret (a hare up to one year old), a hare in flight or even a courting couple — you will have the chance to create a *very* special drawing. Otherwise look for reference photographs in books from which to draw your finest picture.

6

LITTLE FURRY FRIENDS

Work that you have done in the previous chapter will help you learn quickly how to draw some of our smaller furry friends, all of which have a similar head structure to a rabbit.

I paid a visit to a pet shop in order to buy wild bird food but I was distracted for some time by the antics of caged hamsters and gerbils. I asked the proprietor if he would mind me drawing his small charges. He was delighted to know that his animals would appear in this book. It is always wise first to obtain an owner's permission to sketch the creature you want as a subject.

Draw a busy hamster

Inside the pet shop my observations began with a group of hamsters. This charming short-lived animal is a popular pet in schools and homes. The domesticated species are thought to have descended from a pair taken from the wild in a Far East country.

When not asleep hamsters are very busy little animals that seem to hurtle about at high speed. Their tiny hands and feet have five fingers or toes. Sometimes only four are visible. After I had studied their basic shape and noted their fur texture I fixed these in my mind, then jotted down in pencil the outlines of various poses. Details were only put in when I was satisfied with the preliminary drawings. I always work through this method when sketching animals, birds, reptiles, and people! I make no apology for repeating here the crucial importance of going for outlines and proportions first.

Fig. 37   Draw hamsters.

Figure 37 will show you how my technique works. The top example is of a hamster gathering material for its nest. Notice how the body has a big end. See how the skull shape is quite a close likeness to that of a rabbit. Don't miss that short, pointed apology for a tail. The lower sketch depicts a ball of sleeping hamsters. I have used dotted lines, again, to help suggest body form at the outline stage. Hamsters have very short hair which has been suggested by tiny pen strokes and dots. Copy figure 37 in pencil, then in pen.

A hamster feeding was drawn for figure 38. It appeared to be in a hurry to eat. After swiftly filling its cheek pouches with grain it scurried away on the next project — hanging upside down from the cage roof. I used a grade 4B pencil for the basic outline then finished the job with a size 0.1 pen. Draw your version of this example.

Fig. 38 A hamster feeding.

Fig. 39   Draw this gerbil.

Draw a gerbil

My next captive subjects were gerbils. These long-haired mouse-like animals are just as active as hamsters. The wild gerbil is a desert rodent that is nocturnal. Pet gerbils seem to be lively day and night. As usual I had a long careful look at the gerbils before doing any drawing. This is vital preparation before art work can begin — especially when tackling fast moving creatures. Before I began to draw I knew what shape the body, head, legs, tail and ears were. I noted how their long, straggly fur grew, that they had bright black eyes, and the most delicate little hands. This system works for me and it will work for you. Study figure 39 for as long as you want. Without looking at it further, jot down the basic outline. Look again; then draw in the missing details. Do the same exercise with the gerbils drawn for figure 40.

Fig. 40 Sketch these two poses.

Lock up the cat

My house was previously owned by a young lady who kept a dog. Consequently there were no cats about the garden, but there were delightful little wood mice. I first saw one of these animals when I put up a bird table. It popped out to sniff at my shoes. My cat watched it from the comfort of my garden chair.

She did not budge! Kittens which have been taken away from their mothers too early have not been taught to hunt. At this time TC had no idea how to catch her natural lunch, thank goodness. I was able to watch wood mice for several weeks before they were frightened away by numerous cats who soon invaded the garden when TC wasn't around to drive them off. My cat is the undefeated middleweight champion of the area!

Wood mice are common in the countryside and in large gardens which give them shelter and protection from their enemies. They are attractive animals. Their coats vary from pale brown to chestnut with cream chest, chin and belly. Their large ears give them excellent hearing and their sense of smell is good. Figure 41 is a pose typical of this little animal. It sits up to find out what is going on. Notice the oval body shape and a head that is rabbit-like. The long tail is hairless. This is another small friend with tiny fingers and toes. Copy this example in pencil or pen.

Fig. 41 A wood mouse.

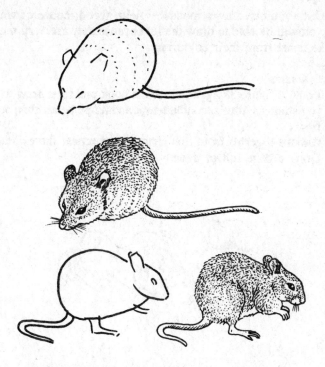

Fig. 42   Use very fine ink marks for depicting fur.

Figure 42 gives other typical mouse positions. Have a go at drawing them. Pencil will be better than pen for depicting the fur texture. Remember to leave a white spot in the eye in order to give it a life-like look, and to put in a few whiskers.

During my schooldays I kept almost anything that moved as a pet. White mice were popular then. These and house mice are very similar to wood mice though grey in colour. I can recall, when working in an office years ago, finding a house mouse in a desk draw where it had made a nest in old files (the best thing for ancient paper!). I fed the mouse on biscuit and bits of sandwich. It soon became tame. I used to look forward to our morning meetings. Then someone reported the matter to Pest Control. Office mice have a hard and short life!

Once you can draw a mouse — field, wood, house or white — you will be able to draw the lot because they are very much alike apart from their colouring.

Assignments
1. Look at figure 38 again, close the book and then draw what you studied. Your second attempt should be better than your first.
2. Choose a gerbil from this chapter and repeat the exercise.
3. Draw a page full of mice.

7

BE FOXY

I live in a large city yet the wild animal I most frequently see is the fox. This elegant, intelligent creature has been around man since the Stone Age. Thousands of years ago it learned that where man was there were likely to be free meals available. Today, as never before, the wily fox has established itself in every town and city. In an urban environment it is safe from the hunt, but victim of motorists. Many are killed on our roads.

Shortly after I took up residence in my house three fox cubs and their parents began to use my garden as a short cut to their earth which was under a tumbledown shed next door. Beyond the end of my patch there are neglected gardens which are covered in brambles and sprouting ash trees. It is a paradise for foxes. I have been able to study and sketch them almost daily.

Draw a portrait of Reynard

The fox got the name of Reynard many hundreds of years ago. The name means 'unconquerable through his cleverness'. It is a very apt title for this resourceful animal which has an ultra-sensitive sense of smell, keen hearing and excellent vision. Farmers hate it on account of their livestock, countrymen hunt it with hounds, but millions of ordinary folk admire it. It is a pleasant sight in our city gardens.

The hardest problem you have in drawing a fox is getting the head to look right. This, of course, is true of sketching most animals. I have included figure 44 to show how to draw a

Fig. 44   A fox in profile.

profile of a fox. Notice the large elliptical ears which have a small kink in the outer rim — similar to that of a cat. The fox has a long pointed snout, large nose, and flared cheeks of white hair. The mask-like face is made more distinctive by dark tear-like marks from the corners of the eyes. This animal is a member of the dog family, but it is like a cat in the way it is agile. Copy figure 44 in pencil.

Figure 45 is what you see when a fox looks at you. City bred cubs and vixens (females) do not seem to have a fear of man like that of a country fox. Those that live in my neck-of-the-woods will let me approach quite near before moving off.

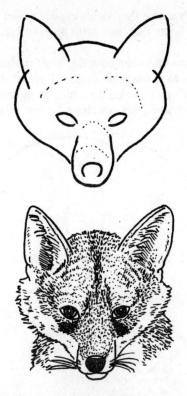

Fig. 45   A fox looking at you.

A frontal view clearly shows the marvellous white fringe round the face. Copy this example in pen or pencil.

Easy poses

On most sunny Spring and Summer mornings I can look out of a bedroom window and see a fox or two basking on a shed roof. They like the sun and will curl up for long spells to sleep in its warmth. Sometimes I have crept slowly and quietly down the garden to get a close up sketch of a sleeping fox but the fox has a sixth sense. The closed eyes suddenly spring open; it becomes fully alert and ready to disappear quickly. Despite foxes being so common in towns many people never see one.

I think this is because they don't expect to see one, and don't look for it. I hope that you will now search your area for Reynard.

Look at figure 46 to see how the basic outline of a sleeping fox is turned into a finished sketch. Lots of dots and dashes again feature. Copy this and then turn to figure 47. This is the view I often get when fox watching. Draw your own version.

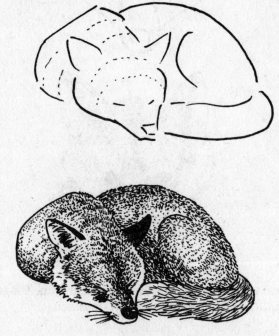

Fig. 46   A still fox to draw.

Chubby cubs

In November and December the nights become noisy with the blood-curdling screams of foxes. It is mating time. The cubs are born in March or April, but it is usually late May before I see the current year's litter. The small chubby cubs are very playful. They indulge in mock fights and affectionately groom each other. When young their fur seems spiky, fine and

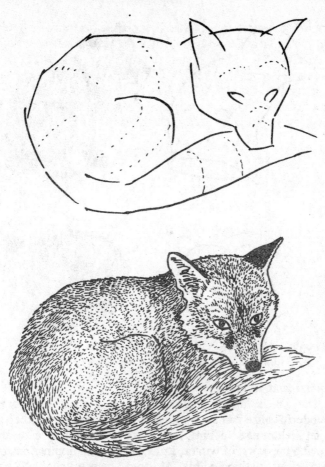

Fig. 47   A fox is quickly alert.

dark in colour. The snout is short and the ears have yet to develop. The tail is short and stubby. Your town or city, like mine, may have a Nature Centre that has foxes. You might be able to sketch them from life as I do. Copy figure 48. You will have to go dotty again (see pages 19 and 120) to draw cubs. Hold your pen lightly so that it just touches the surface of your paper. It takes time but will keep you off the streets!

Fig. 48   Chubby fox cubs.

Hunter and scrounger

The fox is highly intelligent and is a great survivor. Its wonderful nose can soon pinpoint a food supply whether it is a fat fieldmouse, a bird, or a turkey carcass in a dustbin. During the worst of winter, foxes can be seen tipping bins over to rake out anything edible. At dawn I have watched a dog fox nip under the gate of a Primary School, cross a playground, and inspect a row of bins. Litter louts who leave a trail of chips, fish remains, curry and other food about the streets provide the fox with supper. Foxes eat vegetables as well as meat.

I sketched a vixen eating cat food which my over-fussy moggy had left. After she had eaten she turned the dish over. From then on, I always knew when she had been around. Figure 49 is my impression of her feeding. Sketch the basic outline, then draw her.

Fig. 49 A vixen eating cat food.

I don't regularly feed the foxes because they quickly take advantage of the situation. After putting out free meals for them a family of foxes began to visit my garden frequently. They dug huge holes everywhere. The vixen would sit and stare through the kitchen window. It was very interesting, but I had also to consider the safety of my pet cat, TC. While she is young she can take care of herself, but there is evidence that cats that are old, weak or injured are eaten by foxes. I have noted that stray cats tend to disappear when there are growing fox cubs about. Have a look at my drawing of a fox hunting in my garden, figure 50. Copy this. By now you should be quite good, if not brilliant, at animal drawing. It will help you to look back at your early efforts to see how you have improved.

Fig. 50   Draw a fox hunting.

Assignments

1. Choose two illustrations from this chapter, then look at them for one minute. Close the book and draw them from memory after first drawing a basic outline.
2. Draw foxes from photographs.
3. Go out and draw foxes from life — or through a bedroom window!

8

BRIGHT-EYED AND BUSHY-TAILED

The grey squirrel, like the fox, is another wild animal which has taken to our towns in a big way. It is an intelligent, attractive creature which is also a great pest. Despite man it is a resourceful survivor found in many of our parks, woods and cities.

The grey squirrel was introduced a few hundred years ago from North America. It quickly spread throughout the country and was thought to have displaced the native red squirrel. Today this theory is no longer acknowledged by experts. They now think that the red squirrel has become rare because its habitat has shrunk, which is a much more likely explanation.

Just round the corner from where I live there is a busy main road which is lined by tall trees. Grey squirrels build their nests, or drays, in these on a level with the bus's upper deck passengers! If folk are observant they can watch them while on their way to work.

Draw cheeky chops

The grey squirrel quickly learns who it can trust and of whom it can take advantage. Children feed it in parks and gardens.

Grey squirrels frequently pay a visit to my garden to raid the bird food or dig up newly planted flower bulbs. My cat used to chase them into a nearby rowan tree. For a long time the squirrels could always out-climb the cat, but one day she managed to corner a young squirrel in my neighbour's porch. I thought that she would kill the youngster but all she wanted to do was sniff noses with it. From then on the mad pursuits stopped.

You will find that the head shape of a squirrel, which is a rodent, is very similar to that of a mouse or rabbit. You can see this by looking at figure 52. See also the way I have suggested the tail by drawing longish pen strokes which generally radiate around the tail itself. The fur nearest the tail bone is dark grey but this turns to white at the outside. To achieve this impression I have left white space in abundance at the back of the tail. I used short lines which go the same way as it grows on the animal to suggest body fur texture. You will notice that the squirrel has small rounded ears, short whiskers, dark eyes outlined by white or cream fur, long hind legs and toes, and human-like hands. Copy the basic outline first and then draw meticulously in pencil or pen. You might try drawing the tree branch. See how the roundness of this has been suggested by short curved pen strokes. Isn't it easy when you know how?

Always bear in mind when drawing any animal that if you draw the main shape accurately the rest is relatively easy. In other words, *looking* at the overall profile of the pose is more than half the job.

Changing shapes

The grey squirrel, like so many animals, can suddenly change shape dramatically. It is a very agile creature which can climb and bound across open ground at great speed. You may have seen the grey squirrel's intellect featured on television. Scooping up bird food left on a bird table is no problem at all to the enterprising squirrel. However, it is more often filmed, instead, overcoming one obstacle after another in order to get to food. One little fellow who visited my garden showed the same sort of intelligence. I had hung a bag of peanuts on a clothes line. The food was meant to give the birds a bit of help during a cold spell. The squirrel bit through the line then took

Fig. 52 Draw a grey squirrel.

Fig. 53   A hungry squirrel.

its time to eat the spilled nuts. This happened twice more. I then put up a wire line. Did I win? No! Figure 53 is my impression of the squirrel concerned. It scampered along the line upside down then slid down the wire supporting the nut cage. It pulled away the grid and tucked in.

Study figure 53 then copy this in pencil or pen. Notice the flowing lines made by tail and body and how the head is angled out.

The rare red squirrel

A few people are lucky enough to have the rare red squirrel as a garden visitor but most of us would have to explore remote regions in order to see this pretty animal. The one time I have seen it in the wild was on a ramble through a beech wood in the Lake District. The red squirrel is unmistakable. It has a lovely red coat and long tufts of hair on its ears. It is an animal which is found more often in Scotland than in England, where it is confined to small regions of beech wood or coniferous forest. The red squirrel is smaller and slimmer than the chubby grey one. It also has longer fur. The squirrel sketched for figure 54 is in a common pose, sitting up to eat. See how I have drawn the animal and the branch upon which it sits. Copy this example in pencil or pen.

Squirrels are best observed through binoculars while in the shelter of a bush or hide. They are very nervous creatures which move rapidly. They spring from branch to branch before suddenly stopping to listen or look. This is the pose I sketched for figure 55. You can clearly see how the hair radiates from the central bone. This is your next exercise, but scale it up larger than the printed version.

Fig. 54 Draw the rare red squirrel.

Fig. 55   Another view of the red squirrel.

Assignments
1. Study the basic outline in figures 52, 54 and 55. Draw them from memory.
2. Draw a squirrel from a good photograph. Include a bit of the background.
3. Observe and draw grey squirrels from life.

9

DEAR DEER

There are four species of deer which can be found in the wild in our country. We can see them in woodlands, on moors, and in the Scottish Highlands. Because their meat (venison) has become popular, Red deer are also found in deer farms in many parts of the country.

Deer are nervous, gentle creatures which are not too hard to draw once their basic construction is learnt. Deer tend to have powerful bodies supported by thin legs. The male animals grow antlers each year, spectacular by the time they are mature. They shed their antlers, usually in late autumn, then re-grow another pair. They are larger than the females. Fallow deer are the most common deer. However, we shall start by learning how to draw the smallest deer, the Muntjac.

Muntjac deer

The lively, lovely little Muntjac deer is found in woodlands in the South, the Midlands, and the Chilterns. It originally escaped from Woburn Estates, and is slowly increasing its range. It is around 45−48cm tall at the shoulder. The buck (male) has two tiny antlers which are shed late in the year. The small size of the Muntjac makes it very vulnerable to marauding dogs.

Figure 57 illustrates the basic form of both sexes. The top drawing is of the doe (female). I used very fine dot stipple to suggest the short hair. My size 0.1 pen was held very gently and

Fig. 57   Draw our smallest deer.

just dabbed onto the paper for this result. A heavy hand, or slow jabs, do not work for this ultra-fine technique. Copy the examples but draw them out three times the size of the printed sketches.

Roe deer

The Roe deer is common in parts of the Midlands, the North and Scotland and across the South of England. It is about 20cm larger than the Muntjac. Many folk, however, never see a wild deer. This is because they either don't look for them, or do not know where to find them. Deer tend to feed at dawn or

Fig. 58   A Roe deer.

dusk, so it is necessary to go out at these times in order to observe them. I have watched Roe deer enjoying their breakfast in the gardens of a manor house where I teach in the Lake District. These animals are very fond of roses. The manager of this particular house had to fence off his flowers to protect them.

Roe deer damage young trees by rubbing their heads, between the antlers, up and down the bark, presumably to combat itching and to help cast off old antlers. They tend to use the same paths. It's possible to find these in order to spot deer.

Look at figure 58. This is my sketch of a buck Roe sniffing the morning air for his favourite snack. Notice the two small antlers. I watched this animal until it got my scent, then up went its tail, in warning to others, and away it went. Draw your version of this deer.

Fallow deer

The Fallow deer is probably the most often seen of all deer species. These pretty animals can be seen in the grounds of stately homes, estates, parks, zoos, nature reserves, and in woodlands of England, Wales and Ireland. If you visit Richmond Park you may never find any conkers on the ground despite the many horse chestnut trees there are. The various deer there eat up every one that falls, including the prickles. They must have mouths as tough as my old walking boots!

The Fallow deer is a handsome animal easily recognized by the bucks' flattened antlers, called palmated because the shape originally reminded people of the palm of a man's hand. I once came across a buck which had shed one antler. The remaining one was dangling loose as the animal moved. I felt sure that I would soon own a souvenir of the woodlands so I trotted after the buck. After an exhausting half-hour the antler was still attached to the deer which then easily lost me.

Many of the bucks have white spots on their reddish-brown coats. Both sexes have a white patch on the rump, and a black or dark stripe down the centre of the short tail which is held upright as a warning when danger threatens. The Fallow doe has no antlers. She is plain but sweet — this sounds like a description of a friend, doesn't it?

Fig. 59 The basic construction lines for Fallow deer.

Study the basic shapes in figure 59. Draw, in pencil, these construction lines. Remember that once you get the basic shape right the rest is very easy, so you will always end up with a reasonable drawing. Turn to figure 60. See how I have suggested the grain in the antlers, and the texture of the coat. I first pencilled in the spots so that I could ink in the fine lines and dots round them. Then the pencil marks were erased. Now finish off your sketch in a similar fashion.

A popular image

A young Fallow, Roe or Muntjac deer (fawn) has a much loved image. It is used in cartoon films, books, greetings cards, and to advertise commercial products. It has wide appeal.

Fig. 60 Adding the details is easy.

Figure 61 shows examples of the Muntjac and Fallow fawn. Both deer have spots when young, but mostly lose these as they grow to adults. Like many small, baby animals they tend to have large ears and eyes, with fluffy or fine hair.

In late Spring, each year, fawns are born. They are sometimes found by people who then think, because the mother is missing, that the youngster is an orphan. This is almost always a mistake. Mum will know where her baby is. If a fawn is handled by humans it will be deserted by the parents. Young animals, consequently, end up unnecessarily in nature centres, zoos, or being brought up by carers. If you stumble across a fawn leave well alone, assuming it isn't obviously in distress.

Try your hand at drawing a Bambi picture. Begin with a basic construction, then, as before, pop in the fine details with your gentle, controlled hand. There is nothing hard about putting in dot stipple, it just takes a bit of time.

Fig. 61 Draw a pretty Bambi.

Monarch of the Glen

The majestic Red deer stag has been a prized trophy for huntsmen throughout our history. It is still hunted today. You have, no doubt, seen stag heads in stately homes and halls, in museums, and as a background prop on TV and in films.

Their superb adult antlers seem to serve no useful purpose other than as a status symbol. Stags head-butt other males when fighting occurs during the rutting season, although they do not use their antlers as weapons. Nevertheless, don't go near a stag during May or October. You could be charged simply because you have invaded his territory. Some parks have warning notices to this effect.

The quality and maturity of a Red deer stag is usually determined by counting the number of points he has on his antlers. Twelve points indicate a fully grown male which is known as a Royal. A fine beast may have more than 12 points.

Fig. 62   Draw this stag.

Stags and hinds (females) are found on Exmoor, in the South West, the Lake District, and the Scottish Highlands. In addition they are now farmed in many places. You might not like the idea of commercial use of this creature, but it has to be said that captive deer are usually healthier, and live longer than their wild cousins. Their meat is a healthy food, fat free, and has the edge on domestic beef. Our early ancestors depended on this venison until the widespread herds had been greatly reduced. Then Royalty claimed the right to own and hunt the creatures.

Wild Red deer are very wary and soon put to flight, but those in captivity are easily tamed. I used one of these, in a wildlife park, to draw figure 62. This stag browsed by a roadside. I had plenty of time to watch and then draw him. Notice the ruff of long hair round the stag's neck. The antlers have many points growing from a main branch. See how form and shape are suggested by dot stipple. Copy this example.

Assignments

1. Draw from memory the basic shapes of a Fallow, a Muntjac and a Roe deer.
2. Draw from a trophy or photograph the head of a Fallow buck or a Red deer stag.
3. Draw a Bambi as a possible greetings card design.

10

GEE UP

Horses are another ever-popular subject for artists and the general public. We shall work on a few of the scores of different kinds of horse. The much used and abused horse was one of the first wild animals to be tamed and domesticated by man. It has been used for a very wide range of jobs: ploughing, pulling heavy loads, carrying knights in armour and transporting whole armies. Without the mighty Shire horse it is doubtful whether, prior to the advent of the internal combustion engine, we could have fed our population growth as we did. Many elderly people still recall seeing these wonderful amimals working in the fields and hauling heavy loads through our towns.

Horses have been used by man for centuries for riding, hunting, racing, performing, and so on.

The hardest part first

In my opinion, the most difficult part of a horse to draw is the head because the skull is quite complex. It has many small bumps, hollows, ridges and curves. A head from the side (profile) is wedge shaped. See figure 64. Study the way I have suggested bone under skin by using very fine dot stipple. Horses have big eyes, heavy upper eyelids, with long lashes. Their cheeks are prominent, they have a bony ridge down to the nostrils which are surrounded by soft skin. Copy this illustration then move to figure 65. The head from the front is rather like the shape of a coffin. Try to memorize these shapes because then you will be able to draw a horse head from memory. Copy figure 65.

The whole lot

You may be an accomplished horseman or woman and know far more than I about the anatomy of a horse, in which case you should have few problems in drawing a whole animal. We always draw well the things we know best. This is why artists need to learn how things are put together.

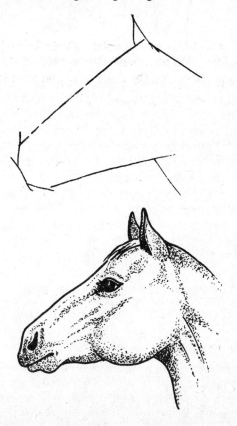

Fig. 64   Use dot stipple to shade in skin texture.

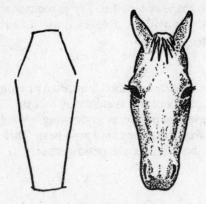

Fig. 65   Coffin-shaped head.

I have had just one riding lesson in my life. A young horse called Rocket was allocated to me. While bouncing painfully along I imagined myself as a famous film star galloping through the Valley of Death. Later, after I had dismounted the frisky beast, someone commented that I was an awful rider. There is all too often a spoilsport around. My horse power has a wheel at each corner nowadays!

My sketch of a horse, figure 66, will give you an idea of the general build of the animal. It will also demonstrate how dot stipple is used to show muscle, form and body shape. It is a most useful, yet simple, technique. Draw this example by starting with an accurate basic construction, then add the details. Be sure to position the eye in the correct place, and note how hooves, tail and mane are suggested.

A good big one

My favourite horse is the gentle giant called a Shire. This immensely powerful animal is one of the largest in the world. Its ancestors were the Medieval Great Horses which were bred in the Midland Shires. Hence its name. For all its size and strength it is a friendly, easily managed animal which is making a welcome return to farms, transport concerns and brewers' dreys.

Fig. 66   Draw an accurate basic form first.

Fig. 67 Draw this Shire horse.

When I was a small schoolboy I once came across a Shire in a field flanked by a dry stone wall. I climbed on top of the wall then struggled onto the broad back of the horse. It didn't seem to mind. We trotted round the field. This exercise was repeated for several days. Then disaster came upon me in the form of an enraged owner who bellowed that the old horse was retired and not up to giving pests like me free rides. We all make little mistakes don't we?

Have a look at figure 67. Observe the sturdy legs, large feet mantled by long hair called feathers, the strong neck, shoulders and massive hind legs. A Shire horse can pull a load of five tonnes with no trouble. Copy this drawing in the usual way.

Wild ponies

The wild ponies on Dartmoor are used to people. Thousands of tourists stop to admire, feed and photograph them. The ponies are small, tough, trustworthy animals who generally like children. The lower drawing in figure 68 is of a Dartmoor pony. Copy this by first drawing out the basic shape.

The upper sketch in figure 68 is my drawing of an Exmoor pony. This is rare compared to the Dartmoor pony. I have seen this animal mixed up with a Red deer herd. In the winter the Exmoor pony grows a thick coat of hair. After walking those moors in January I know that it has the right idea! When summer comes it moults to a thinner coat. What a wise animal. This pony is stronger and sturdier than the Dartmoor species.

Work out the basic shape for each of these wild ponies; then complete each one in pencil or pen.

Draw an action horse

It was not until the camera was invented that the action of a running animal became evident to us. When a cine-camera film could freeze the fast-moving legs of a horse, for example, artists and others knew for the first time how to get their drawings right. For centuries artists had tended to sketch and paint running animals with their front legs out and the hind legs stretched back in a similar way. When we look at pictures of Victorian hunt scenes, for instance, we see horse, hound and

Fig. 68   An Exmoor and a Dartmoor pony.

fox all depicted in this strange position. The movement of animals was, of course, too quick for a human eye to follow, hence the mistake. Three cheers for the camera!

In actual fact there is a cycle of many different positions for the legs of a horse to be in when it runs. There is one point in a gallop when the animal is balanced on the point of one hoof. I have illustrated just three positions of a galloping horse for figure 69. Study these before copying them. It would help you to draw to a larger scale. Then you could finish off with dot stipple, and perhaps a bit of background, flying turf, and a fleeting shadow.

There is close-up action in my drawing for figure 70. This was drawn from a photograph about which there is more in the last chapter of this book. Notice the way movement can be

Fig. 69   The action of a horse running.

depicted by the horse's flying mane and the way the jockey is crouched forward with one hand on the reins whilst the other clutches a whip. There is a suggestion of a brush fence with bits of it dislodged as the horse jumps over it. Draw your own version of my drawing.

Fig. 70 Over the sticks.

Assignments
1. From a newspaper photograph draw a race horse. Put in a suggestion of the background.
2. From life or a good picture draw a working Shire horse. Include in your picture a background to depict a farm or similar environment.
3. Draw a wild pony as a possible design for a birthday card. Think about a suitable background and then draw it in.

11

FARM ANIMALS

Fig. 72   A British Friesian cow.

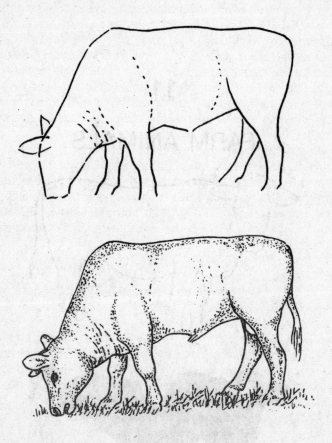

Fig. 73   Draw this young bull.

Once upon a time there were thousands of little farms which carried a range of farm animals. Today we have the era of the huge agricultural complex which tends to specialise. We can still find a variety of farm animals in one place, however, in nature centres, parks, and on some wildlife estates.

Cattle

One of the commonest beasts around our countryside is the cow. I see more black and white British Friesians than other breeds. The Friesian is a docile animal. Cows are usually curious about what humans are up to. They will stand still and look at you. See figure 72 of a cow who was doing just this when I stopped to draw her. See how the basic outline defines the sagging belly, slightly curved spine, coffin-like head shape, large ears, sturdy legs and deep chest. Try to fix in your mind the distinctive form. I used a small paint brush and black ink to fill in the markings.

If you want to draw a bull from life do not take chances. They can be temperamental. The animal I drew for figure 73 seemed to be gentle and unconcerned about me, but I worked from behind a wire fence just in case it wasn't. It was a huge beast with a cream coat, very short horns and strong shoulder muscles. See how dot stipple has been used to depict the power of the bull. Draw your version of him.

Giddy goats

Did you know that we have wild goats in certain parts of our country? No? Nor did I until I became a rambler and discovered wild, or feral, goats in Snowdonia. They were nimble enough to leap from rocky hill ledges into the tops of trees in order to chomp leaves for their lunch. If I had not seen this spectacular event happen I would not have thought that it was possible. Wild goats can also be found on stretches of the Somerset coast. They tend to be larger animals than the tame variety. Feral goats have dark, shaggy coats and wicked looking horns that could give you a nasty prod!

The friendly goat drawn for figure 74 was admired and fussed over by a party of children who were learning how to draw. It was partial to sweets, crisps, apples — and drawing paper! The male, or billy, goats have horns; the females do not. All goats have oblong eye pupils. Copy the sketches in figure 74.

Fig. 74 A friendly creature to draw.

Bacon on the hoof

There are pig farms all over the place so seeing pigs, before the poor things become bacon, is quite easy. I like watching these intelligent creatures despite their smell. They seem to be forever hungry and constantly searching for food over which they tussle noisily. The pig is quite comical and much used by cartoonists. Study the pig drawn for figure 75. Notice the blunt snout, huge ears which shade small eyes, the silly, curly tail and small trotters. I used tiny dashes and dot stipple to depict the strange hide. Draw a serious or funny sketch of a pig.

Fig. 75 The ever-hungry pig.

Cluck cluck

Birds which we commonly see are dealt with in detail later on in this book, but you may care to start on birds by looking at the exotic farm fowl, which I have chosen to test your considerable skill. While it is nice to see an increase in free-range chickens, most of these brown, stubby birds are kept for the number of eggs laid, and are not as attractive to draw as the fancy fowl which I have drawn in figure 76. I came across these birds in a nature centre. Rare birds such as these are making a come-back from the old days of chicken keeping and showing.

The striking design on the feathers of the cock bird here consists of wavy, dark grey marks on a white background, which are particularly suited for pen work. See the odd way the tail feathers grow; some sprout across the base of the tail,

Fig. 76   Free range fancy chickens.

and there is one feather, longer than the rest, which has a white stem ending in a sort of arrow design at the tip. The cock has a fine, impressive comb and large wattles hanging down below the sharp beak. Before you start to copy this bird have a look at the way I have drawn the basic form of a hen. The dotted lines help to give an illusion of roundness in the bulky body. The hens of this species have golden-coloured mantles and dark brown markings against a reddish-brown background. The stout tail feathers are almost black. I have shaded these in my drawing. When you copy these birds sketch the construction lines before putting in all the time-consuming detailed markings.

There are many more friends on the farm, such as geese, turkeys, mules, donkeys, calves, and others which I have not been able to cover in this chapter due to the problem of having too many subjects but not enough pages. There are none, however, that you cannot draw with great skill following the methods you have learned so far.

Assignments
1. Without looking at figure 72 draw a Friesian cow. Check your result.
2. Carry out a similar exercise with a pig.
3. Draw chickens from life or photographs. Add in background details.

12

WOOF, WOOF

Dogs are unique animals. All they seem to want from us is love, affection, food and shelter. While millions of people keep dogs there are many owners who do not understand dog behaviour. Folk do not realise that this popular creature has strong pack instincts. If the owner is not the pack leader then the dog will take over this role with sometimes disastrous consequences. The modern trend towards keeping potentially lethal guard dogs all too often proves this point. Most household pets, however, are delightful little chums who are faithful, loyal, good company and fun.

I have made dogs the last exercise in drawing four-footed friends in this book because you need to observe so very accurately before starting to sketch. Unlike domestic cats, dogs come in all shapes and sizes. All dogs do not share the same type of skull. Some have deep foreheads while others are streamlined, stubby, long or whatever. There are so many different breeds that I can cover only a few of them.

Start with heads

One of my favourite dogs is the Border collie. This wonderful sheep controller is very popular and has been made more so by television series which feature sheep dog trials. I once owned a city-bred collie which was a great pet, but not trained to round up anything other than me! He was full of energy, very friendly and good to be with.

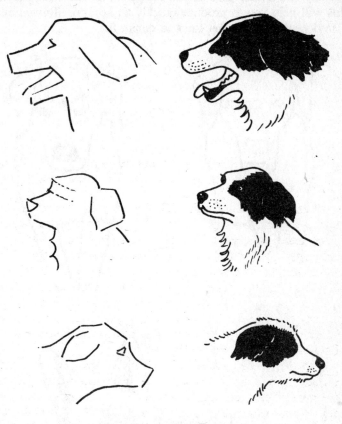

Fig. 78   Profile heads.

Look at my drawings of two adult dogs and a puppy in figure 78. Notice how well defined the foreheads are and the long snouts. I have left a white line round part of the ears so their shape can be seen. The black markings, which are quite black on these animals, were put in with a brush and black drawing ink. Copy figure 78 by starting with the construction lines, as shown; then the little details added in become easy. The front views of heads in figure 79 are slightly more difficult but not beyond your talent. See how the eyes are drawn

between the dotted lines. If you use pencil for the basic sketch
this will help you to produce quickly an accurate illustration.
Use dot stipple and tiny lines to depict fur.

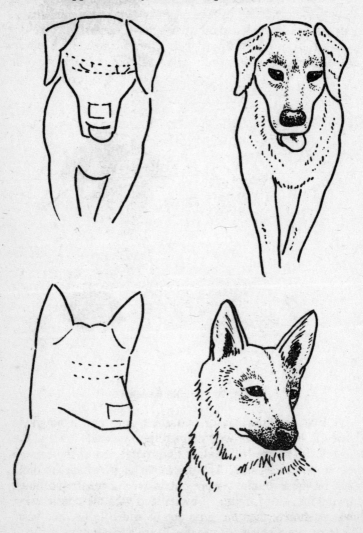

Fig. 79 Draw heads to start you off.

A bit of action

Thousands of people are fascinated to watch the way sheep dogs work. The collie, for example, seems to control sheep fully by simply fixing its eyes on them. The sheep immediately look worried but do exactly what the shepherd and the dog want — if they both know their jobs. I have drawn Border collies stalking and dashing after sheep for figure 80. The

Fig. 80 Typical poses.

Fig. 81   A Cocker Spaniel.

sketches were done after first drawing several quick pencil roughs then working on the best of them with a pen. Try this system. Copy figure 80. Begin with building a basic shape for each animal. Then, when you are satisfied, finish your gem with your pen.

Another dog seen on television in trials is the Cocker spaniel, which excels in scenting out and retrieving game birds. Some of these highly skilled animals are worth a small fortune for their remarkable ability. They are intelligent, obedient creatures who make good pets when not plunging through undergrowth. Study the sketches in figure 81. You will see that I have used a controlled scribble to show the dark brown coat markings. Notice how *much* white I have left showing through. Copy these illustrations in your usual way by starting with a sound basic shape.

Assignments

1. Draw an accurate profile and a front view of your favourite dog.
2. Try to sketch three different breeds of dog. Work from life or photographs.
3. Draw your fast impressions of a dog moving. Use pencil or pen.

13

FEATHERED FRIENDS

Having worked through this book your observation and drawing will be good enough for you to tackle bird art. Depicting our feathered friends requires keen vision, attention to detail, a good memory and ability with pen or pencil. That means you, doesn't it?

Many beginner artists think that birds are much too difficult to sketch because they rarely stay still for long, so they never attempt this fascinating subject. I once thought the same way, but became hooked on identifying the birds around me. I read many books and guides on birds, became increasingly interested in them and then began my art by copying photographs, drawings and specimens in museums. You can begin by copying my ink illustrations. Try using a 2B pencil to make things easier. My complete drawings here in this chapter have close ink shading but you can use very fine pencil lines and then smudge them with your finger to produce a wide range of lovely grey tones.

Heads, beaks and bodies

Bird watching is a very popular hobby for thousands of people. These keen folk are sometimes called 'twitchers'. A good twitcher can identify a bird in seconds. How is it done? It is a bit like aircraft recognition. The watcher learns about body, head, wing shape, and a lot more, including habitat, colour, flying characteristics, feeding habits, song or call and so on. A would-be bird artist follows the same route – and takes on a new, interesting hobby which can become a nice little earner!

Fig. 83 **Different heads and beaks.**

Figure 83 shows the head and beak differences between just four kinds of bird. The top four drawings are of a peregrine falcon. Under this is a duck, then a seagull and at the bottom a member of the finch family. Notice how beak shapes differ. Most artists tend to draw birds in profile because they are easier to identify from this angle. Copy these examples in pencil. Start by drawing the basic shape accurately.

Fig. 84   Simply drawn body shapes.

When I want to draw a bird I first take a good look at the overall shape of it. I then jot this down before adding beak, eye, and wing details. It is a construction job. Figure 84 is an example of this. Copy these and try to sketch them quickly. With a little practice you will soon become good enough to draw some birds from memory even after only a fleeting glimpse.

Certain birds which can be seen feeding along sea shores are called waders. One handsome little fellow, a redshank, was the subject for figure 85. Notice how simple these fast impressions have been kept. See how a bird can stretch or contract its neck,

Fig. 85 Fast sketches from life.

Fig. 86   Draw this swan.

and the way it uses its long legs. Try to extend your skill by studying figure 85 for two minutes then jotting down what you saw. This is excellent practice for drawing from life.

Recently, when watching birds on Derwentwater in the Lake District, I saw an angry male swan attack and kill a large duck. The poor duck was grabbed by its neck then held under water until it drowned. Not content with murder the swan swung the corpse round and round for five minutes. Swans are well known for defending their mate, young or nests, but in this case the swan seemed to be totally alone on the lake. These impressive birds all belong to the Queen. Maybe the one I watched will end up in the Tower of London! When swans are on guard they are rather like a battleship cruising into action. I drew one like this for figure 86. I used a fine pen for putting in the feather detail. Always remember to leave a white spot in the upper eye. This keeps the swan awake! Draw your version of this swan.

Fig. 87 Common garden birds.

Little dinosaurs in the garden

Birds are now thought to be the only living relatives of dinosaurs because they have a similar bone structure, are warm-blooded, lay eggs and make nests. Maybe it's just as well that the garden variety are small. Who would fancy daily feeding of huge flying monsters? In this country the most common bird must be the humble sparrow which is a handsome little chap. Figure 87 has one at the top, with a greenfinch in the middle and a chaffinch at the bottom. I have drawn wing and feather details to show you how they fit together, but it's not necessary to put in all these items when producing fast sketches from life. The amount of such detail

Fig. 88   A thrush and a blackbird.

which you can see decreases with distance. Notice how the three species seem to look alike, but a close study reveals slightly different wing, tail and beak formation. Try drawing these birds twice the size of the printed ones. Start with a correct basic shape and then add in the bits and pieces.

Those of us who have a garden may frequently see a thrush or blackbird searching for a tasty worm or two. These two birds are alike in build but totally different in colouring. While writing this I am able to watch a mother blackbird collect insects for her young which are in a nest close to my window. From time-to-time I rush out into the garden to scare off a marauding cat, magpie and/or the occasional squirrel. All are enemies of young garden birds. Copy the examples in figure 88.

There are many kinds of bird feet. Take a look at figure 89. The top left foot is that of a perching bird. These make up the majority of our feathered chums. The foot, bottom left, is that of a golden eagle. This has to be strong with sharp talons to hold and kill prey. The top right drawing shows the foot of a woodpecker. This has evolved so that this bird can grip to bark tightly while it hunts for insects or hammers out a nesting hole.

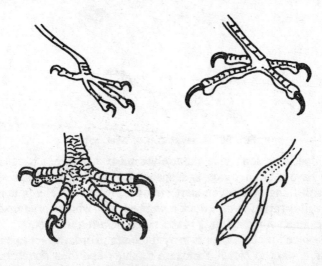

Fig. 89   Birds' feet.

Fig. 90 A selection of seabirds.

Woodpeckers don't give themselves nasty headaches because they have a brain which is suspended in liquid. You learn all sorts of things when you start out as a bird artist! The bottom right illustration is of a duck's webbed foot which, of course, is designed for paddling. Make notes of different feet.

It's nice for city dwellers to visit the sea in order to see exotic birds. I went to North Yorkshire to study and then sketch the birds you can see in figure 90. All these birds, plus hundreds more, were on the same crowded cliff face in the Royal Society for the Protection of Birds reserve at Bempton. It was nesting time. The gannet, top sketch, is a large bird with a wing span equal to the height of a tall man. It makes spectacular high speed dives straight into the sea when fishing. The razor bill, middle left (not to the same scale), hunts in a more sedate fashion. This is a darkly marked bird with white wing flashes. The little puffin, middle right, is a charming creature that is much persecuted by killer gulls and other predators. It has a large, multi-coloured bill for scooping up tiny sand eels. The gentle-looking bird at the bottom of figure 90 is a kittiwake. This pretty creature spends most of its life on the wing so it was great to be able to see it at close quarters. Notice the black-tipped wing and tail feathers. Scale up your drawing to copy these fine birds.

Quackers

You need go no further than your local park pond, lake or stream to sketch the birds in figure 91. The top illustration is of a mallard duck coming in to land. Note the way it fans out its tail to act as a brake. It can also reverse the thrust of its wings to slow up. A handful of old bread crusts will soon bring a flock to you. You may have noticed that it is the male birds which are the most colourful or striking. This is because the females tend to be drab so that they blend in with their environment when nesting. Nature isn't silly is it?

Small dark birds are often to be found where there is water. The middle drawings of figure 91 are of a coot and a moorhen. People sometimes confuse the two. The coot, middle left, is a black bird with a white forehead and light beak. It is slightly larger than a moorhen, which has a red beak and legs, and white wing flashes with white under the tail, as in the drawing middle right. The tufted duck, bottom drawing, is black with white underparts. Draw your version of figure 91.

Falcons

Falconry is now a popular sport. It is possible to see some magnificent birds of prey in reserves and zoos. Some garden

Fig. 91 Birds of pond, river and lake.

centres now have the added attraction of a falconry which may contain a wide collection of birds of prey. There is one little falcon, however, which all who use our motorways can see every few miles, though drivers mustn't allow themselves to be distracted from the road. The kestrel is the bird which hovers

Fig. 92 Draw this kestrel.

over motorway verges as it hunts for voles and insects. It is a very attractive creature. Look at the male kestrel I have drawn for figure 92. I sketched in each main feather shape before shading it in with close lines. Then the black markings were put in, with dot stipple used for the head feather markings. You can make a nice picture of this by using a soft pencil. Most bird pictures, by the way, are much better done as paintings, but before you can paint you need to learn how to draw your subjects accurately. Copy the kestrel.

Flighty

Experienced bird artists can recognize some birds by the way they fly. I have drawn six different birds in flight for figure 93.

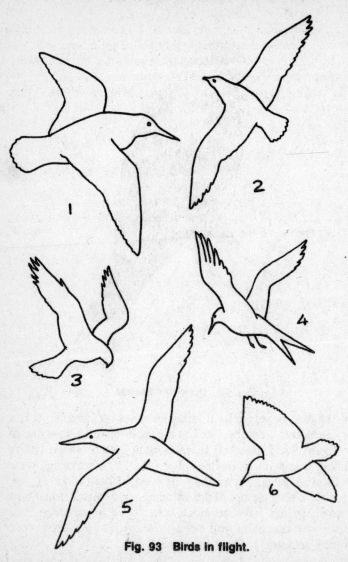

Fig. 93 Birds in flight.

Number 1 is an oyster catcher. This is a black and white bird which has a red beak. I'm surprised that it is called an oyster catcher because oysters only form a tiny proportion of its diet.

2 is a kittiwake; 3 a hovering kestrel; 4 a common tern (I once visited a nesting site of this highly active little bird — it was on a freezing cold wet day which gave me quite a turn!); number 5 is a sketch of a gannet scaled down to fit in here; and 6 is one of a woodpecker. Try sketching these interesting shapes.

Assignments
1. Draw a garden bird from life.
2. Observe a bird in flight and then jot down in your sketch pad your impression of it.
3. From life or a photograph, draw a bird portrait.
4. Sketch birds in their natural environment by drawing in suggestions of the background.

14

ODDS AND ENDS

Sometimes it is necessary to use photographs in order to draw certain subjects. Working from a photo does not mean copying it exactly. More often than not, photographs lack the composition or clarity which an artist may need. The aim should be, therefore, to use the information which a photograph can give. It is like a writer using a dictionary.

Scaling up or down

Before you begin to work from photographs I will explain how to scale up (enlarge) a drawing and how to sketch from a large picture. It's a very useful device to have handy and one that is used by commercial artists.

You will require a sheet or two of clear plastic of the sort used with overhead projectors. On this you mark a grid with the aid of a rule and a black pen. Start with a grid of 1cm squares. This is the one to lay over the photograph or drawing that you wish to work from. Your next task is to draw very lightly in pencil another grid onto your drawing paper. You can make this of 2cm squares − if you want to double the size of the image in the photo. Then you simply transfer, square by square, what is in the photograph to your drawing paper.

Figure 95 is my example of scaling up, to double size, a picture of a Roe deer. The top illustration shows the small grid, the lower sketch shows the basic lines drawn out in pencil on the larger grid. When satisfied with this operation I inked over

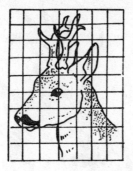

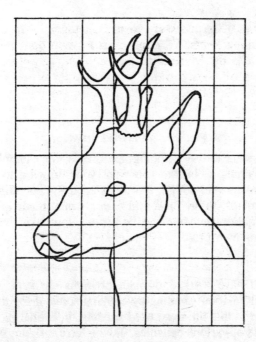

Fig. 95 Make a grid.

the pencil lines and when they were dry erased out any which
showed, together with the grid lines. The last job was to finish
off by putting in the details. See the complete drawing in
figure 96.

Fig. 96   A finished drawing.

If you want to use a photograph that is, for example, twice or more times as big as you want your drawing to be, you would make a grid with 2, 3 or 4cm squares, depending on the measurements, to lay on it and then a pencil-made small grid of 1cm squares on your pad or paper. Now take time out to make your own grid.

Shading

As you have worked through previous chapters you have learnt a little about shading by copying some of my drawings. I have found that the most used shading, in animal pictures, is dot stipple of various densities. Take a look at figure 97. I have used a pen size 0.5 and 0.1 to make the top sketches. The finest dots are obtained by the way you use your pen. For this you use a gentle grip and just lightly dab the paper. For stronger dots you simply increase the pressure of your fingers or use a larger size of pen.

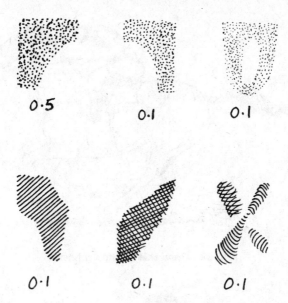

Fig. 97 Useful shading techniques.

The shading in the lower half of figure 97 is close-line shading. This can be used vertically, diagonally, curved or whatever, in order to give you the effect you want. Just remember to keep all the lines the same distance apart and, usually, running the same way. The darkest patches or shade are best done with cross-hatching, as in the middle drawing.

Great action drawings

Newspaper shots of subjects in action are great to use. I drew the racehorse in figure 98 from a daily paper sports page. The original showed a group of horses, but I selected just one to draw. Notice how a streaming tail and bits of flying turf help to convey action. You might try scaling this up twice when you draw your own version of it.

I enjoy sketching horses, so I turned my attention to another one for figure 99. The newspaper depicted a dark horse jumping against a background of dark hedge. For my drawing

Fig. 98   Draw this galloping horse.

Fig. 99   Use shading to help your drawings.

I made the horse pale and subdued the hedge. I then put in a little shadow on the ground and over the hedge to show the horse better. Shadows are another useful device for artists. Scale up figure 99 for a bit more practice.

One of my favourite animals is the highly intelligent dolphin. This mammal (warm blooded) has always been man's great friend but, sadly, all humans do not return this friendliness. Some fishermen still hunt it, while others kill it in drift-netting used for tuna fishing. Other dolphins become performing prisoners in sideshows and marine parks. The dolphin must be a very forgiving animal!

Fig. 100   A jumping dolphin.

The bottle-nose dolphin drawn for figure 100, however, was photographed enjoying a natural life in the ocean. See how its jump is captured by a curved body, explosion of water and spray of drops, as the dolphin is about to plunge back into the sea. Note the way I have used shading to suggest waves and dot stipple for the skin texture. Scale up and draw your own version of this charming creature.

Animal portraits

When you consider drawing an animal portrait keep in mind that you need to isolate the subject from a complicated background. Often, the best work is one that concentrates solely on the animal's head, expressive eyes and character. A portrait of a bird, however, is perhaps more attractive if the whole bird is drawn with, maybe, just a hint of its environment put in.

Several years ago I had a spot of beginner's luck when I photographed a tame eagle owl. My snapshot was good enough to draw, paint and sculpt from. I have used it again to draw another portrait of this magnificent bird of prey featured in figure 101. It was a large specimen with golden eyes and a pale chest streaked with black and brown markings, some of which were rather like a herring bone in shape. The head, body and wings were mixed shades of mottled brown against a cream background. An owl has four toes. It will sometimes perch with two toes forward and two back. The one illustrated had three toes forward on one foot and two showing on the other one.

If you ever handle an owl you will find that it feels just like the softest silk. This is because its feathers are particularly light and covered by fine down on the underside. It has evolved this way to enable it to fly silently when hunting. A deaf wood mouse stands no chance against it!

The eagle owl is quite common in zoos, parks and some garden centres. See if you can draw figure 101 three times the printed size. To do this would need a 1cm grid on my sketch and 3cm squares in light pencil, on your pad.

The grey wagtail, drawn for figure 102, is an attractive bird

Fig. 101 Scale up this eagle owl.

which is found near rivers, streams and lakes, where it feeds on water insects. It has a blue grey head and back, yellow chest with a black bib, black and white wings and tail, and white flashes above and below the eyes. I used dot stipple shading to suggest shadow on the rock and to fill in part of the bird. Reflections in the water have been depicted by short, wavy lines of different widths. Scale this drawing up to about twice the size of the printed one.

Fig. 102 Draw a grey wagtail.

Pet portraits

Baby animals and domestic pets make good portraits and are very popular pictures. Become good at this skill and you can earn money with it. People will almost always pay for a good likeness of their favourite pet.

The lamb and young rabbit in figure 103 are ideal for drawn portraits. Notice how shadow is used to pick out the face and bone structure beneath the fur. See how you get on by scaling them up for pencil studies. A larger size will enable you to put in more of the coat detail.

Fig. 103 Baby animals make popular pictures.

I could not resist drawing a portrait of a Basset Hound. This gentle, affectionate dog is a popular pet which has been made famous through films, television and strip cartoons in newspapers. Despite its rather sad-looking face this animal has great physical stamina, and an excellent nose which can be used to track deer, hare or rabbit.

See figure 104. The wrinkled forehead, face and long, drooping, velvety ears help to give it a worried image. Take a note of how the coat has been drawn. The deep-set eyes have a patch of pink skin (haw) showing beneath the eye-ball. Carefully study all the details before drawing, first lightly in pencil, then in ink, your version of figure 104.

A final word

It has not been possible to cover all animals in this book, but I hope that the ones you have practised drawing will encourage you to portray any creature on our planet. Good luck to you.

Fig. 104   Draw a Basset Hound.